I spy with my little eye, something shining in the sky. It's a star! A star shining over Bethlehem.

I spy with my little eye
glittering gifts of gold
frankincense and myrrh.

Look! There are three camels with
wisemen carrying glittering gifts!
Gifts, they say, for a special baby.

I spy with my little
eye something grey.

It's a donkey with
Mary and Joseph! They
are on their way to
Bethlehem.

I spy with my little eye something crowded.

It's an inn! An inn full of people! Mary and Joseph have nowhere to go.
But God has a special plan.

I spy with my little eye
something extraordinary.

It looks like the kind innkeeper
is leading Mary and Joseph
somewhere.

I wonder where that will be?

I spy with my little eye
something glorious!

It's Angels in the sky!
Singing peace on earth
and goodwill towards men.

I spy with my little eye something woolly.

Sheep! There's lots of sheep with shepherds too. Look! The Angels are speaking to the shepherds.

I spy with my little eye something wondrous.

A crowd in the stable!

The wisemen, shepherds, sheep, donkey, Joseph, and Mary, are gathered around a manger in a stable.

I spy with my little eye something very precious.

It's baby Jesus lying in a manger!

The wisemen travelled from afar guided by a star; Angels spoke to the shepherds and there was no room at the inn for Mary and Joseph. But God led them all to a very special baby. Jesus, Emmanuel, God with us.

It was all part of God's
very special plan.
Glorious indeed!

As you ponder over the Christmas season, I pray this book would be a guiding resource as you share the birth of Jesus with your little ones. May you remember the truest form of love come down from above to save us all.
Merry Christmas!

For unto us a child is born, unto us a son is given: and the government shall be upon his shoulder: and his name shall be called Wonderful, Counsellor, The mighty God, The everlasting Father, The Prince of Peace.
Isaiah 9:6 KJV

www.ingramcontent.com/pod-product-compliance
Lightning Source LLC
Chambersburg PA
CBHW041409160426
42811CB00106B/1562